40 SONNETS

by the same author

poetry
NIL NIL
GOD'S GIFT TO WOMEN
THE EYES
LANDING LIGHT
ORPHEUS
RAIN
SELECTED POEMS

prose
READING SHAKESPEARE'S SONNETS
SMITH: A READER'S GUIDE TO THE POETRY OF MICHAEL DONAGHY

aphorism
THE BOOK OF SHADOWS
THE BLIND EYE

editor (selected)
101 SONNETS
ROBERT BURNS: SELECTED POEMS
DON'T ASK ME WHAT I MEAN
(*with* Clare Brown)
NEW BRITISH POETRY
(*with* Charles Simic)
TRAIN SONGS
(*with* Sean O'Brien)

DON PATERSON

40 Sonnets

FABER & FABER

First published in 2015
by Faber & Faber Ltd
Bloomsbury House
74–77 Great Russell Street
London WC1B 3DA
This paperback edition published in 2016

Typeset by Hamish Ironside
Printed in England by Martins the Printers, Berwick-upon-Tweed

A CIP record for this book is available from the British Library

ISBN 978-0-571-31091-3

2 4 6 8 10 9 7 5 3 1

For Nora and Frances

Acknowledgements

I am grateful to the editors of the following publications, where many of these poems first appeared: *The Blinking Eye*, *Contemporary Poetry and Contemporary Science*, *Elsewhere*, *Granta*, *Guardian*, *Hiding in Full View* (with Alison Watt), *Jubilee Lines*, *London Review of Books*, *New Yorker*, *New York Review of Books*, *One for the Trouble*, *Ploughshares* and *Sunday Telegraph*. I would also like to thank the National Gallery, Bristol Festival of Ideas, Edinburgh International Book Festival/ McSweeney's, Cambridge *Thresholds* project/Whipple Museum, and the Arden Bloomsbury Shakespeare 400 project, who commissioned a number of these poems. I am indebted to Matthew Hollis, Nora Chassler and Nick Laird for their meticulous comments.

Contents

Soy un habitante, pero ¿de dónde?
— ANTONIO PORCHIA

Here

I must quit sleeping in the afternoon.
I do it for my heart, but all too soon
my heart has called it off. It does not love me.
If it downed tools, there'd soon be nothing of me.
Its hammer-beat says *you are*, not *I am*.
It prints me off here like a telegram.
What do *I* say? How can the lonely word
know who has sent it out, or who has heard?
Long years since I came round in her womb
enough myself to know I was not home,
my dear sea up in arms at the wrong shore
and her loud heart like a landlord at the door.
Where are we now? What misdemeanour sealed
my transfer? Mother, why so far afield?

Wave

For months I'd moved across the open water
like a wheel under its skin, a frictionless
and by then almost wholly abstract matter
with nothing in my head beyond the bliss
of my own breaking, how the long foreshore
would hear my full confession, and I'd drain
into the shale till I was filtered pure.
There was no way to tell on that bare plain
but I felt my power run down with the miles
and by the time I saw the scattered sails,
the painted front and children on the pier
I was nothing but a fold in her blue gown
and knew I was already in the clear.
I hit the beach and swept away the town.

The Air

What is this dark and silent caravan
that being nowhere, neither comes nor goes;
that being never, has no hour or span;
of which we can say only that it flows?
How was it that this empty datastream,
this cache of dead light could so lose its way
it wandered back to feed on its own dream?
How did that dream grow to the waking day?
What is the sound that fades up from the hiss,
like a glass some random downdraught had set ringing,
now full of its only note, its lonely call,
drawing on its song to keep it singing?
When will the air stop breathing? Will it all
come to nothing, if nothing came to this?

The Eye

The empty mind you finally display
ten weeks into the yogic agony
of your silent retreat, you will discover
in the latter stages of a gin hangover.
So too the self you slaughtered in the bliss
of her astonishing astonished kiss,
the loch in starlight or the late quartet
is what your dog knows as its waking state.

All I mean is *soul* just can't allude
to that pretty trance you might know twice a year
when the ape is somehow home enough or mind
is lost enough for both to disappear,
but what it leaves unguarded and unblind.
Its holocaust. Its vast solicitude.

A Pocket Horizon

The idea, I guess, is on the kind of day
the vapours are sent down to blind and choke us
one still might gain some distance, much the way
this shotglass seems to give me a little focus
or this stone in my shoe some foothold on events.
Its disc of jet on three gold screws would do
for a doll's house table at a doll's house séance.
I'm trying to what exactly. Level with you?

Chin down on the bar-rail and one-eyed
to get it true and straight and down to scale.
But my red eye looms above its tiny tide
and my breath is screaming like a winter gale
I think there's no one on the other side
O love where is my white or my black sail

Radka Toneff

I'll let you go, if you'll let this come good.
I'm speaking it as quietly as I can
a mile or so into the Bygdøy wood
where you lost your voice. So much for the plan
to *master the sounds closest to silence, sing
piano*. Though I know now what you meant.
When the ear lights on the half-said thing
it leans into its distance, and is sent
out into those spectral fires that play
between the inner world and outer dark
as we are, to this zone of breath and blue
between the world and the dark. Radka, skylark,
you rose too far; though as it died away
I heard right through the song to what sung you.

The Six

for John Abercrombie at 70

You still sound like that man in early middle age
whose demolition firm went west and marriage south,
who was looking at his birthday through a fifth of Jack
when all his friends pitched in to buy him a guitar.

Two months it sat in silence. Then one day he found
that he could play whatever came into his head.
And such was his surprise each time he picked it up,
he couldn't hear himself above the sounds he made –

the six strings still below his fingers, like a novice
or like Orpheus, who would not let them thrill
with selfhood, lest it place a wall before the temple.

Each night he reasons out the things he'd say to her
and the song he plays is sad, because it's now too late,
and joyous, as somewhere the heart has yet been won.

'House'

Better, all in all, the god we know –
broken, drunk, in agony, at bay,
yet undistracted from the mystery
of our own suffering; and if they show
it's last, to blunder wild-eyed through the screen
with *Stop the chemo! He just needs to fart!*
or gently intimate it might be smart
to swap your Tolstoy for a magazine.

We too have known that three o'clock abyss
between the differential and the kiss
where a man must face the smaller man within
or remember where he stashed the Vicodin.
O let that thousand-yard-and-one-inch stare
see through us too; for we don't have a prayer.

The Big Listener

for Tony Blair

Midnight. Connaught Square. A headlight beam
finds Cherie just back from her speaking date.
She looks at you. Less animal of late.
You lose no sleep, but wake within a dream.
Your favourite: that old divided dark,
the white square at your neck; your good ear bent
towards the long sighs of your penitent.
You rinse a thousand souls before the lark
and wake refreshed, if somewhat at a loss
as to why they seem so lost for words.
They are your dead, who still rose to the birds
the day we filled the booths and made the cross,
before you'd forced them howling to their knees
to suffer your attentions. Spare us. Please.

A Powercut

This is what we've come to, this damn lift,
this blackout, this airlock, this voiceless stop,
this empty set, this storm cave, this dead drop,
this deaf nut, this dumb waiter, this blind drift,
this Necker cube, this coalshed, this Swiss bank,
this iron lung, this hide, this diving bell,
this pseudocoma, priesthole, holding cell,
this meatlocker, this isolation tank,
this, since I'm too lazy for the stairs in
this airless guesthouse in the Dales, so went for
this jackscrew for the old or lame or spent for
this two-second trip between two floors, this
this-way-up box to sweat and say my prayers in,
this six-foot night, this theatre of doors: this.

The Self-Illuminated

i.m. Peter Porter

As your hand turns white upon the book
we'd biked across so you might see it done,
only you could – at a time like this –
put me in mind of that rum business
with St Fillan of Glen Dochart, whose brief entry
in the *Breviarium Aberdonense*
tells of the stone he spat when he was born,
and how, denied a candle in his cell,
he found his left arm light up from within
so he could read, till sleep turned out his skin.
His relics are five: the carved head of his crook;
his once-candescent bones; his flying bell;
and two long lost – one, perhaps his psalter,
the other a manuscript, or a portable altar.

Funeral Prayer

Today we friends and strangers meet
because our friend is now complete.
He has left time. Perhaps we feel
we are the ghosts and him the real –
so fixed and constant does he seem,
so starlike. May the human dream
arise again to find him woken
at its heart, though to be spoken
once is as miraculous
as a thousand times. What utters us,
blind nature, told the trees and birds
and bright stars; yet of all the words
we knew, his name was the most dear.
We give thanks he was spoken here.

At the Perty

efter Ishikawa

Jack
clapped
Ma

t'
ma
back

left –
richt –
left –

stapped

grat

she
's that
licht

clapped – attached; *stapped* – stopped; *grat* – sobbed; *licht* – light

Lacrima

For years, I'd begged him for the smallest word.
Finally I cursed him with the worst I knew.
Silent skies. Maybe it was true,
and he never was? But then I heard
his breath behind my own; even in his sleep
he brooded on the form my hell might take.
So I forgave him. O that shook him awake –
he raged and howled; then he began to weep.

One drop belled at the fracture in his side,
and then a stream, a flood, a tidal race –
all he was was one huge tear. In his place
there stood a human shape cut from the void,
an empty tearless glory. I walked in
and now I wear it like a second skin.

Francesca Woodman

i

At the heart there is a hollow sun
by which we are constructed and undone

ii

Behind the mirror. Favourite place to hide.
I didn't breathe. They looked so long I died.

iii

What's shown when we unveil, disclose, undress,
is first the promise, then its emptiness

iv

Ghost-face. Not because I turned my head,
but because what looked at me was dead.

v

– We don't exist – We only dream we're here –
This means we never die – We disappear –

vi

We'd met 'in previous lives', he was convinced.
Yeah, I thought. And haven't spoken since.

vii

All rooms will hide you, if you stand just so.
All ghosts know this. That's really all they know.

Two

These two, if two, can only half-exist,
their being so lost, so inwardly inclined
that were somehow the universal mind
to make its inventory, they would be missed,
their bodies having slipped between the hours
and dropped down to this silent underland,
the white torque of their sheet still in her hand
like the means of their escape. From the light purse
of their mouths, they pass their only coin
endlessly, so none may buy or sell.
Each has drawn so long and drank so deep
from the other's throat or root, they cannot tell
tongue from tail or end from origin.
Sleep would halve them so they will not sleep.

A Vow

When I was ruined by love, I took a vow
that if I loved again, I'd love the less;
so when I spoke love, spoke it to excess,
as love will make its mirror anyhow.
But I talk to myself, and late one day
Love heard me crowing of my secret share
and taxed me all the false love I'd declared.

Now I feel nothing but her stream away
the way she does, dead slow and fast as light
like a galaxy that leaves behind one spark
too low and dull to catch her silent drift;
though somewhere out there in my turning dark
they know each sunrise falling like a lift
and the white curve of her arm gone from the night.

A Threshold

Where have you gone, my little saving grace?
Iona or Iola of the laugh
like falling silver . . . Now nothing's in its place,
and all's as light and cold as that blue scarf
I lost or left without, or I don't own.
Everything shames me. Every card declined.
You slid between the stalls and you were gone
though I scoured the field for hours, hoping to find
you sat with 'the silent children of the fair'
or some such nonsense, though I always knew
you'd taken another hand, the way kids do,
not looking up. This place again. It's where
I wake up and recall I have no daughter
or fall asleep and dream I have no daughter.

The Foot

'Mowing the Grass', Gaza 2014

I have no words so here are the no words
for one who was playing football on the beach
when you shelled it for kicks, and whose father
while the medic 'frantically works away'
strokes his gawky long-toed sockless foot
– the boy is eleven or twelve, at that age kids
suddenly start to grow overnight – then 'playfully'
pinches his toes one by one, then lifts the foot
and lets it drop the way an ape might do
then stroking the foot again 'weeps quietly'
and 'smiles as he recalls some happier time'
but 'seeing the doctor shake his head' grips the foot
with both hands and 'starts to howl like an animal'
as 'the full horror of the situation dawns on him'

Seven Questions about the Journey

Why are we leaving in such unreadiness?
– *Your name was last*
Is it too late to call? Is there still time to confess?
– *The moment's passed*
If the weather is stormy, should we go nonetheless?
– *None forecast*
Where are the dogs and the horses? Should we guess?
– *Slain. Shot. Gassed*
How will we know when we reach our new address?
– *Heed the blast*
How do we look in our fine new leaving-dress?
– *Alone. Aghast*
Where are we going, so light and riderless?
– *Nowhere. Fast*

Fit

A girl lies in a field of flowers.
A sea of tiny milk-stars pours
out of her head, from every limb,
pours off the star she makes in them,
the star-shape that she'll leave behind
some other wandering child will find
and fit themselves as she had done
into the day's eye of the sun.

Back there a boy lies where he fell.
How long he's lain he cannot tell
but he is bored with his review
of dirt and roots and wants it through.
Fit your four limbs to his stain
you'll find you cannot rise again.

The Version

after Nicanor Parra

Like many of my colleagues, I too received the envelope
of dark green card bearing the green-and-gold stamp
of their far-off land, and the handwritten invitation to
contribute a new poem to be translated for the five-
hundredth edition of their journal, which would contain
nothing but foreign poets in translation. The Slovenian
business was still fresh in my memory, and I'd rather
have hacked off my hand at the wrist than see my work
diminished in that manner again. But the mortgage pay-
ment was looming, and their line-rate was impossibly
generous . . . So I conceived of a brilliant plan. I would
write a poem *about* translation, designed to lose precisely
everything in translation – such would be the density
of its idiom, the baroque recursion of its argument, the
depth of its lyric intrigue. (Its subject, or at least such
part of it as could be paraphrased, was the creation of a
poem so volatile it would burst spontaneously into flames
before it could be read.) 'The Version' would consist of
my biographical note and photograph, opposite a blank
recto carrying only an apology from the editor. My
notoriety would be instantaneous. I daydreamed . . .
From that day, I would be known in their land as 'The
Silent Poet' . . . My blank books would be set texts at
their universities, and I would be flown to their stadia
to not read to thousands. I sent off my only copy of the
work, with a firm request that they destroy the original
after the translation was made, for The Silent Poet leaves
no trace. As I'd predicted, a succession of their own

poets ducked out of the task, claiming everything from migraine to the sudden deaths of close family members. But rather than give up, they passed it on to some professor of Stylistics. Being one of those smartasses whose game is to make something of anything – of absolutely nothing, if necessary – it seems he read my barely moving lips, and drew his conclusions. (Whether he had intended to honour my request to shred the original or not is irrelevant: we can assume my poem was lost when a flunked student of his turned arsonist, and razed his house to the ground.) When they sent me my author's copy of the journal – assuming, correctly, that I did not know one word of their raucous, glide- and liquid-free tongue – they thought 'I might be interested to know' what their man had made of it.

I ascertained that this reverse translation had been made by some chap who mostly worked on software manuals. The rendering as prose and consequent loss of my immaculate alexandrines I could have foreseen, but as far as I could recall, my original sonnet bore no relation to this poem in any way whatsoever. However, what animated me most at the time – I now find this hilarious – was its facile *mise en abîme*, and its rather blokey and ludic tone, given I'd quit doing that sort of thing fifteen years ago. And then the real horror began. A friend alerted me to the fact that someone had submitted this garrulous bullshit to some magazine *in my name*. When I wrote to the editor to protest, she angrily referred me to three other journals where 'The Version' had *also* appeared, each time in a completely different form: one is violently pornographic, and directs the reader towards a

number of illegal sites on the dark web; another accuses (in virulently anti-Semitic terms) another poet, by name, of fucking his own sister; another yields an acrostic insulting the prophet Mohammed . . . My increasingly hysterical protestations fall on deaf ears. Within a week, I hear that I have been dropped from several reading lists, that a Nobel laureate is suing me for plagiarism, that a series of public readings has been cancelled . . . Now my work is returned from journals unopened, my agent has dropped me, and yesterday I received an email from my publisher saying *under the current circumstances we cannot in all conscience continue to support your work.* While I dwindle, 'The Version' proliferates. I am writing this in the cupboard below the stairs, and the banging on the front door has stopped; I think they are in the house now. A yard away, a man with a voice I half know has just spoken my name. I cannot let him hear me breathe.

The Fable of the Open Book

Once upon a time there was a book.
The book lay open to a page. The page
had a margin, and they shared a dirty look –
though the truth is they were practically engaged.
The page said roughly what it thought it should,
the margin said exactly what it wanted,
and all was grand. But one thing spoiled the mood
of the wee verge. 'I'm so squished and tiny-fonted!
Why the hell should *that* guy hog the floor?
I'll shove that silly bigmouth out the door!'
And soon the page was lying in the gutter.
Now it could weep and wail, and spit and splutter!
'Time,' the margin cried, 'to make my mark!'
And suddenly it went completely dark.

To Dundee City Council

Fair play. Round here, only junkies walk
so it's unfair that I affect my shock
at this last straw: that fine baronial stair
you found cheaper to fence off than to repair,
thus adding twenty minutes to my trip
via ringroad, bombsite, rape tunnel and skip
to the library where poor folks go to die
or download porno on the free wifi.

My shameful vanity? I thought you might
take time, this time, to personalise the slight.
Know at least I leave here with my tail
between my legs again, and setting sail
for that fine country called the fuck away.
Farewell! Good luck with the V&A.

An Incarnation

Hello? Yep Uh huh Speaking This is he
The householder, aye Uh huh Yeah I'm free
to speak right now How long'll this thing be?
What sort of message? From what agency?
Yes No No I can't 'confirm my identity' –
I *know* I'm me – Eh? Hang on you called *me*,
so you tell *me* my name, and then we'll see –
Yeah This is he Aye Donald Just one t
No, no middle name Yep DOB –
October thirtieth nineteen sixty-three
Macalpine Cougan Never naw Dundee
I guess White British? None No I agree
 Agree Agree I strongly disagree
 You what me? *Hold*? For how long? Seriously?

 Jesus. Speaking speaking This is he

Requests

O tell us more about your dad,
or why your second wife went mad,
or how it was you had no choice
but to give those men a voice;
sing that Cornish lullaby
you hush your kids with when they cry,
produce a boiled egg from your pocket,
a flageolet from your jacket,
expand on your idea that rhyme
is dead, or tell us of the time
you dropped your cellphone in the toilet;
a joke, a bird-call – please don't spoil it,
go on with your brilliant proem!
Anything but read your poem.

For a Drowned Poet

after Du Fu

An October wind
has cleared the sky

and the brown waters
clarify their depths.

What might one reflect
in this empty hour?

When will the wild geese
bring their high word?

I whisper with one
fool enough to choose

perfection of the work.
How hell rejoiced.

I mail this poem for him
into the river.

Le Joueur d'Échecs

In films, the end will come as a surprise
one move after the move you loudly name
in that long-outmoded fashion that implies
you're in a film, or this is your first game.
Then the child or drunk or talking duck
will hold your gaze as they declare you mated,
whereupon you learn what fools call luck
is only what was not anticipated.

In life, we tip the king. We call that class.
But not you, friend: no, you stuck to the plot
to walk me later past the cameras
and down the platform to the X-marked spot . . .
Yet here we are, the back rank of the Vic,
your white throat in the dark, the silent flick.

A Scholar

Pro captu lectoris habent sua fata libelli

The light is dying, and the clock has died;
the page succumbs to the atrocious care
that disinters the things not wholly there
by which your solemn field is justified.
You burnish them until they bear the shine
of common knowledge, knowing one black skill
is yours alone: before the greater will
all text is dream, and takes on the design
of what was sought there. Thus your word is god.
This grammarie electrifies the gate;
none pass but such as you initiate.
The students hurry by you in the quad
attending to their feet. What can you say?
You know your Shakespeare would have walked that way.

Little Aster

after Gottfried Benn

We hauled the drayman onto the slab.
He'd drowned in the canal. Some wag
had set a small blue flower between his teeth.

When I went below his skin with my long knife
and reached up along through the chest
to cut out the tongue and the soft palate

I must have touched the stem and dislodged the thing;
it'd slipped from his mouth and into the brain
I'd set beside him in a steel bowl.

I packed the flower with the woodshavings
back into his empty chest
and stitched him up again.

Drink your fill of that great vase!
Sleep well, my little aster!

Shutter

As she slept
 late
 below
 the naked
skylight
he lapped
 her breast
sky-blue

 had she blinked
 at the crow
 or rook,
 some four-square
 burst
 of the dark?

Apsinthion

What did I do in the war?
Son, I watched a download bar
and drank the last thing in the house.
I ran the show on meshugaas
the way some ancient dynamo
we couldn't replace would only go
on walnut oil or cherry must.
My poems sucked. My guitar grew dust.

But when we heard the star would fall,
did we choose to die like sheep?
Hell no – we were *men*, and blessed
to know the hour and place . . . I jest.
One by one we fell asleep
and that is how they found us all.

Nostalgia

I miss when I could drop down on all fours
and flick the ground away from under me.
I miss the wire I ran into the earth.
I miss when I was the bloom on the sea
and we slept forever under the warm clouds
till something spoiled in us twitched with design
and woke the clock. So we arose and went.
Last night I rowed out to the beeless glade
and lay down on the grass to listen
to the water eating at the edge of things.
My sister taught me to watch the stars this way
lest I think that heaven was up, or heaven,
lest I forget the stars are also under us
where they sink and sail into the dark like cinders.

A Calling

vellet abesse quidem, sed adest
– OVID, *Metamorphoses*, III

A winter train; a gale; a poacher's moon.
The black glass. Do I honestly still blame
the wrong turn in the changing rooms I took
when I was six, and stood too long to look?
The roar Miss Venner loosed at me: 'The *nerve*!'
I was ablaze. And it was worth the shame,
or so I thought, though it was far too soon
to tell the dream from what I'd paid for it.
Then soon too late. Two sides of the same door.
Was it her bow's recoil or its release
that lashed the world so out of shape? Tonight
I stare right through the face that I deserve
as all my ghost-dogs thrash along the shore,
the dark sea at their back like the police.

Sentinel

for Nora

Those times when you advance on me like a statue
holding the plain truth in a bowl of fire,
I will think of you, aged six and running
from that two-room ark, your brother's lonely rage
to where your father would not be again, brushing
the pot seeds from your coat, your moon-white hair,
figuring *someone round here needs to pay some*
 fucking attention
as you tack across a Broadway gridlock, in the dark
 and rain –
then the day I lost you in Kings Cross at rush hour
and saw *I* was the lost one, lost in the roiling,
polyhedral sea of their desire –
then found you on the edge, with all in view,
all in hand, tall as a mast of white pine
to which I had to lash myself or drown.

On Woodman's Photography

for Durs Grünbein

art
A secret game: that's always how its starts.
And best you don't know what you're playing at.

debut
Thirteen. Hairhead. World's eye on a string.
Guess which way I'm looking? *Wrong! Wrong! Wrong!*

technique
To shoot your own ghost, gentlemen – a primer:
locked room; open shutter; fucked self-timer

show
Within my hourly frame, a three-voiced song:
torque, tension, gravity. Thus am I hung.

formula
As frame from reel, as second from the day
we are not symbol but synecdoche

focus
'The lens is no one looking back.' No doubt,
but watch me watch me stare the bastard out

speed
Every thirty seconds, one more mile.
So we all go. The rest is down to style.

Séance

S p e k e . – s e e s s k s e e k
i e i k s e s s e - . - e s k k s e – s s k
p p p p p i - … i – – i i i ´ – s k
k s p s p e i … i i i s s s k p
p s p p i s . . ´ . e s k s s i i i s i s p
k p p p i s s k i i s – k p s p i k e s p s e
s s s s p s p i k e i – s s e i . . – e i – …
s s k s p i i k s e s . . i –
k s e s s s – – k k k s e . i e e i e k e
k s e e i i s s i p i s e e - e s e i k p k i
s s s k p – i k p s p i k e i i i – p i p k i p
k i i i k s e k i p p i k e – – e s i i s k
k i . k s s s i s s s i k i i e e s k e i s s k –
i s s s k s s k p i i i k s p s p p p p p

Souls

The body is at home in time and space
and loves things, how they come and go, and such
distances as it might cross or place
between the things it loves and its own touch.
But for you, soul, whom the body bred in error
like some weird pearl, everything is wrong.
Space is stone, and time a breakneck terror
where you hold to nothing but your own small song.
No wonder you would rather stay asleep
than wake again to your live burial.
But sometimes, shrinking in your tiny keep
you make out through the thousand-mile-thick wall
the faint tapped code of one as trapped as you:
saying: *those high white mansions – I dream them too –*

Mercies

She might have had months left of her dog-years,
but to be who? She'd grown light as a nest
and spent the whole day under her long ears
listening to the bad radio in her breast.
On the steel bench, knowing what was taking shape
she tried and tried to stand, as if to sign
that she was still of use, and should escape
our selection. So I turned her face to mine,
and seeing only love there – which, for all
the wolf in her, she knew as well as we did –
she lay back down and let the needle enter.
And love was surely what her eyes conceded
as her stare grew hard, and one bright aerial
quit making its report back to the centre.

The Roundabout

for Jamie and Russ

It's moving still, that wooden roundabout
we found at the field's end, sunk in the grass
like an ancient buckler from the giants' war.
The first day of good weather, our first out
after me and your mother. Its thrawn mass
was like trying to push a tree over, or row
a galley sealed in ice. I was all for
giving up when we felt it give, and go.
What had saved the axle all those years?
It let out one great drawn-out yawn and swung
away like a hundred gates. Our hands still burning
we lay and looked up at a sky so clear
there was nothing in the world to prove our turning
but our light heads, and the wind's lung.